Hello, Family Members,

Learning to read is one of the most important accomplishments of early childhood. **Hello Reader!** books are designed to help children become skilled readers who like to read. Beginning readers learn to read by remembering frequently used words like "the," "is," and "and"; by using phonics skills to decode new words; and by interpreting picture and text clues. These books provide both the stories children enjoy and the structure they need to read fluently and independently. Here are suggestions for helping your child *before*, *during*, and *after* reading:

Before

- Look at the cover and pictures and have your child predict what the story is about.
- Read the story to your child.
- Encourage your child to chime in with familiar words and phrases.
- Echo read with your child by reading a line first and having your child read it after you do.

During

- Have your child think about a word he or she does not recognize right away. Provide hints such as "Let's see if we know the sounds" and "Have we read other words like this one?"
- Encourage your child to use phonics skills to sound out new words.
- Provide the word for your child when more assistance is needed so that he or she does not struggle and the experience of reading with you is a positive one.
- Encourage your child to have fun by reading with a lot of expression . . . like an actor!

After

- Have your child keep lists of interesting and favorite words.
- Encourage your child to read the books over and over again. Have him or her read to brothers, sisters, grandparents, and even teddy bears. Repeated readings develop confidence in young readers.
- Talk about the stories. Ask and answer questions. Share ideas about the funniest and most interesting characters and events in the stories.

I do hope that you and your child enjoy this book.

—Francie Alexander
 Reading Specialist,
 Scholastic's Learning Ventures

For Kim, my favorite author,
with love
— K.S.

To my mother, Clara Jo
— J.C.

Text copyright © 2001 by Karen Shapiro.
Illustrations copyright © 2001 by Jean Cassels.

All rights reserved. Published by Scholastic Inc.
SCHOLASTIC, HELLO READER, CARTWHEEL BOOKS and associated logos
are trademarks and/or registered trademarks of Scholastic Inc.

Library of Congress Cataloging-in-Publication Data

Shapiro, Karen.
    Butterflies / by Karen Shapiro; illustrated by Jean Cassels.
        p.   cm.—(Hello reader! science Level 2)
    "Cartwheel books."
    ISBN 0-439-20636-7
        1. Butterflies—Juvenile Literature. [1. Butterflies.] I. Cassels, Jean, ill. II. Title. III.
Series.

QL544.2.S47 2001
595.78'9—dc21   00-035783

12 11 10 9 8 7 6 5 4 3 2 1   01 02 03 04 05

Printed in the U.S.A.
First printing, April 2001

24

Butterflies

by Karen Shapiro
Illustrated by Jean Cassels

Hello Reader! Science — Level 2

SCHOLASTIC INC.

Cartwheel
·B·O·O·K·S·®

New York   Toronto   London   Auckland   Sydney
Mexico City   New Delhi   Hong Kong

See the butterfly up in the sky.
Watch it as it flutters by!

Butterflies start as tiny eggs.

Out come caterpillars with
many legs.

Little caterpillars growing long,
crawling,
feeding,
getting strong.

They love to nibble and to chew.
They eat small leaves
and big leaves, too.

Four weeks pass. They grow more.
They shed their skin.
One time,

two times,

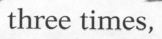

three times,

four.

Once again a change comes around.
Now it is hanging upside down.

Soon,

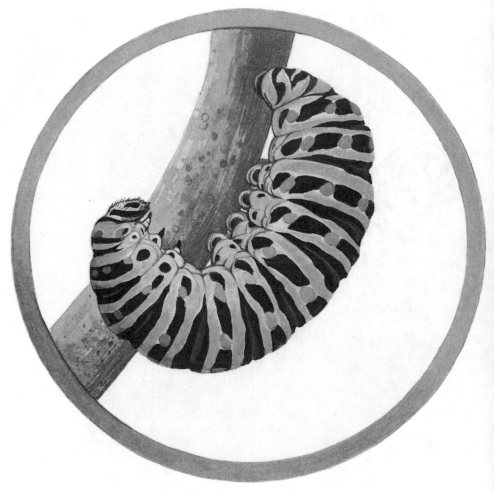

it spins a silky pad
to hold on tight,
and a halter, too,
to keep it upright.

Now it sheds its skin
one time more,
to reveal a chrysalis,
not at all like the skin before.

15

Inside this shell it is changing,
growing.
Eyes, legs, wings,
are now almost showing.

What can it be?
Wait and see.

It's a butterfly!

Its wings are wet.
It has to rest.
It can't fly yet.

Soon, it tries hard with all its might,
spreads its four wings —
and takes flight.

Like a flower in the sky,
what a sight —
a butterfly!

Wings of black, orange,
yellow, and blue,
red, green, gold,
and purple, too.

Colors bright as in a rainbow.
What makes these colors?
Do you know?

It's layers of little scales that we see.
They make the colors as
bright as can be!

Butterflies drink nectar from
pretty flowers.
It tastes so sweet, they sip for hours.

They use their long, thin tongues
to drink.
That's kind of odd, don't you think?

From caterpillar to butterfly
takes eight weeks in all.
All sizes of butterflies —
big and small.

See the butterfly up in the sky.
Watch it as it flutters by!